Aquarium Guides

Looking After Tropical Fish

Kevin Wilson

Luminescent Media

Looking After Tropical Fish

Kevin Wilson

Text and design © 2013 Luminescent Media

Find us on the web at www.luminescentmedia.co.uk
Contact us on office@luminescentmedia.co.uk

ISBN-13: 978-1484904053

ISBN-10: 1484904052

Table of Contents

Basic Equipment

Aquariums

Choosing a tank is mostly personal preference, however, it is a good idea to try buy the largest tank you can afford and accommodate. It also depends on the type of fish you want to keep. For example if you wanted to keep larger fish such as clown loaches you would need a 300-500L tank. If you wanted to keep platys or guppies then anywhere from 30L to 90L would be a good size.

Above: A good tank for larger fish, eg loaches, plec, cory etc

Good tanks 10-80litre for small fish to medium sized fish: eg tetras, neons, guppies, platies etc.

A typical tropical aquarium setup.

If you plan to keep larger fish (eg more than 6 inches) then 250litre+ is a good size. Makes a stunning addition to any living room and should be positioned where it can be seen and appreciated.

Think carefully where the tank will be positioned as it weighs a ton when completely full and would be virtually impossible to move later.

Always make sure you get a cabinet that is specially designed to support your size aquarium. Water is very heavy and a tank positioned on an unstable cabinet is dangerous and can collapse.

Filters

Internal filters stick on the inside wall of the aquarium and are suitable for small to medium sized aquariums.

External canister filters sit in the cabinet under the aquarium and have pipe work running to and from the tank. These are best for large tank setups.

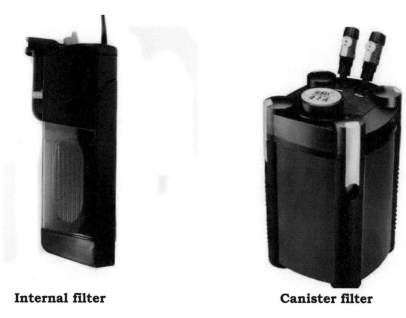

Internal filter   **Canister filter**

For best circulation, place your filter on the back wall toward the right hand side as shown below.

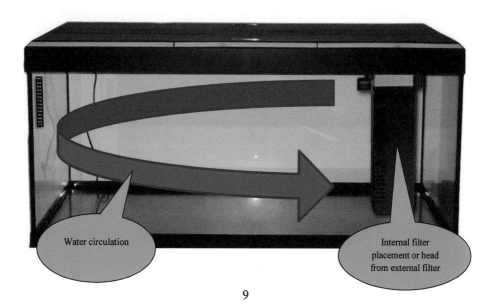

Water circulation

Internal filter placement or head from external filter

What's Inside the Filter?

The inside of your filter will consist of sponges that remove particles of solid waste and also contain some kind of biological media such as ceramic rings or chips.

Some smaller filters only contain sponges.

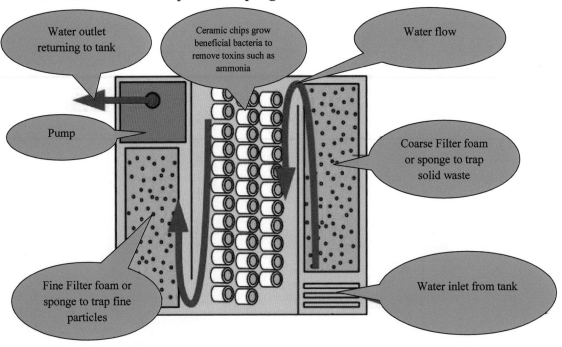

Filter media, ceramic bio rings that promote growth of beneficial bacteria to neutralise toxins such as ammonia. Also filter sponges that trap solid and fine waste.

What Size Filter?

The packaging will tell you what aquarium size the filter is capable of supporting. Look for a filter that is capable of running a tank at least as large as yours, ideally a bit bigger.

If you keep messy fish, such as goldfish or cichlids, or a tank with a lot of fish, you'll need to consider something bigger – the next filter model up.

Below is a table of rough recommendations for filters according to tank volume. I have used the Fluval filters in this guide but any equivalent filter will be sufficient.

Tank Volume	Filter
50ltr	200ltr/h (eg Fluval U1)
66ltr	400ltr/h (eg Fluval U2 or 106)
85ltr	400ltr/h (eg Fluval U3 or 206)
105ltr	700ltr/h (eg Fluval U3 or 206)
120ltr	700ltr/h (eg Fluval U3 or 206)
150ltr	1000ltr/h (eg Fluval U4 or 306)
200-300ltr	1200ltr/h (eg Fluval 306)
400ltr	1400ltr/h (eg Fluval 406)
500ltr	2000ltr/h (eg Fluval FX5)

Heaters

As a general guide you should have at least 1 watt per 1 litre. So a tank that holds 200 litres (52 US gallons) should be equipped with at least a 200W heater.

What Size Heater?

Below is a table of rough recommendations for heaters based on tank volume

Volume	Heater
50ltr	50w
66ltr	100w
85ltr	100w
105ltr	100w
120ltr	100w
150ltr	200w
200ltr	200w
250-300ltr	300w
400-500ltr	2x300w (one at each end)

The water in the tank is subject to room temperature variance meaning if your tank is in a cold room, you may need to go for the next model up as you will need more power to keep the water up to temperature.

For best circulation put the heater on the back wall on the opposite end to the filter.

Lights

To provide enough light for plants to grow and for the fish to feel comfortable, the aquarium should be lit between 6 and 10 hours depending on plant and fish species. Don't keep your lights on for more than 10 hours as this can cause a lot of green algae to grow. Try to turn the lights on and off at the same times each day to try to simulate a tropical day.

Fluorescent Tubes.

T8 tubes are considered standard lighting, if you have a planted aquarium or have a deep aquarium you would need several T8 tubes.

T5 tubes are the brightest fluorescent lighting available but because of this they will also use more electricity and the tubes also get hotter.

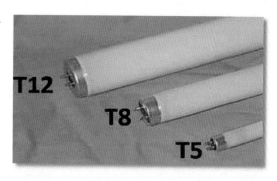

LED Lighting

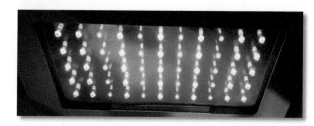

LEDs are cheaper to run as they don't use as much electricity and they come in a wide range of colours, do not emit much heat. Some LED flexible lighting strips that can be used to create a moonlight.

Simple Lighting Example

Type of tubes: 2x T8s or 2 T5 (depending on size of tank) but this should work up to a 4ft tank.

Type colour: Natural daylight (eg life-glo)

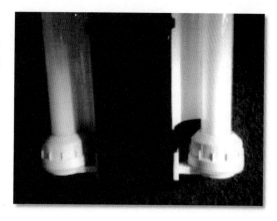

A popular make of aquarium lighting is the Glo Fluorescent Bulbs they produce bulbs for different purposes

Sun-Glo – general purpose lighting, few fish artificial plants
Life-Glo – simulates the strong midday sunlight. This is good for plant growth
Aqua-Glo – intensifies the colours of the fish and also is good for plant growth
Flora-Glo – this is good for planted tanks as it promotes good plant growth
Power-Glo – is good for all purpose tanks and good for plant growth.

The choice of bulbs greatly depends on what you have in your tank. Eg, Aqua-Glo and Power-Glow for a planted tank with lots of fish.

The specs on the bulbs should have a wavelength peak in the red band (650nm), the blue band (around 400nm) to promote plant growth, and to intensify the fish's colours a peak in the yellow band (around 500nm) and between 5500k and 7500k.

Tip: Don't just turn the lights on from dark, this will startle the fish, turn on the room lights or open curtains first, let the fish adjust to the change in light levels

How Much Light?

As a very rough guide, best plant growth will be provided.

Low lights are between 1 - 2 watts per us gallon (0.3 - 0.5 watt/litre)

Medium lights are between 2 - 3 watts per us gallon (0.5 - 0.8 watt/litre)

High lights have 3 watts per us gallon or higher (0.8 watt/litre or higher)

For example

250 litre tank @ 0.3 watts per litre. 250×0.3=75w. I put 2 40watt T8 bulbs in my lighting strip giving me 80watts of light which is enough for most aquatic plants on the market.

60 litre tank @ 0.3 watts per litre. 60×0.3=18w. An 18w-20w T8 or T5 tube will be sufficient. Remember to measure the length of your tank to make sure the lights fit – especially for smaller tanks and non-rectangular tanks.

Remember this is only to give you a very rough idea and is not exact.

These calculations are also useful when choosing aquatic plants as many of the pet stores quote light requirements in watt/litre or similar.

Siphons and Pumps

Siphon and gravel cleaner

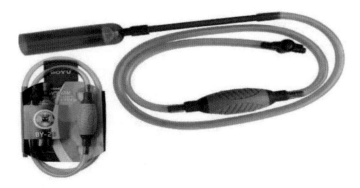

Siphon up muck into a bucket from gravel at bottom of tank while changing water

For large tanks a water pump to pump the prepared and conditioned water back into the tank.

Water Conditioners

There are a lot of water conditioners on the market but I have found that API Stress Coat works well with tropical fish. Water conditioners are designed to make tap water safe for fish. Water companies add chlorine or chloramine to kill pathogens and bacteria in the water to make it fit for human consumption. Unfortunately this isn't good news for fish as chlorine, chloramine and some dissolved heavy metals are toxic to fish, so it's vital to buy a good water conditioner.

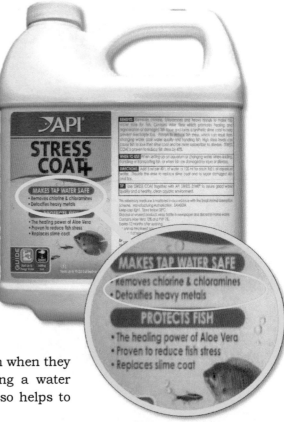

When buying a conditioner make sure it neutralises chloramine and chlorine as well as heavy metals from the water, this will usually be stated on the label.

Some conditioners have extra agents that help the fish. Stress Coat contains aloe vera and helps reduce stress in the fish when they have been transported or disturbed during a water change or tank maintenance. Aloe vera also helps to heal gills and fins.

It is also a good idea to keep some ammonia and nitrite remover in case of emergencies especially when your tank has not been running very long.

When you add fish it is possible to get an ammonia spike until the filter bacteria compensates for the extra bioload.

Only use ammonia or nitrite remover if fish are severely stressed and you have performed a water change.

Rocks & Décor

You can pick up a nice selection of artificial rocks, caves and interesting objects from your local fish store. These can look very real when surrounded by live plants, bog wood and rocks.

Little rocks and caves provide plenty of shelter and hiding places for the fish. This makes them feel more secure in their environment.

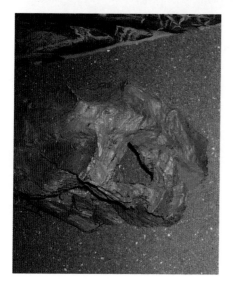

Loach tubes are great for bottom dwelling fish such as loaches, plecos and corys. They love to hide in the tubes. Can you see the loach's nose in the bottom tube? He loves it.

Substrate & Gravel

The choice of gravel and substrate depends greatly on the type of fish you want to keep and whether you want to keep live plants or artificial. I would strongly recommend live plants as it has a lot more benefits to the aquarium than artificial plants.

For bottom dwelling fish you would be better with a fine substrate.

Fine sand is not recommended for live plants as it compacts the roots cutting off nutrients and can cause problems.

For live plants it is good to put it down in the tank in layers. The first layer could be something like Eco Complete Planting Substrate which contains Iron, calcium, magnesium, potassium, sulphur plus over 25 other elements.

This contains all the mineral nutrients needed for luxurious aquatic plant growth without nuisance algae. It will not increase pH or carbonate hardness. No artificial dyes, paints or chemical coatings. Encourages the most vibrant colouration in fishes and reduces stress. Supplies calcium without raising pH. Contains live Heterotrophic bacteria to rapidly convert your fishes waste into natural food for your aquatic plants.

Tetra Plant Complete Substrate is another substrate specially formulated planting medium, for long-term fertilisation. Creates ideal environment for aquatic plants, ensuring long-term release of key nutrients. Contains high quality mix of sand and black peat, with high iron and trace element content. Optimum grain size for rapid development of healthy roots. Free of nitrates and phosphates to prevent algae growth

There are plenty more on the market but I find either of these ones are fine for the bottom layer

For the top layer, this is personal choice but I would recommend a dark brown fine gravel with 1mm grains. This will give it the most natural look and will show up the green plants well against the dark brown gravel. For example JBL Manado. Any fine gravel or course sand will do.

Fine gravel is also much better for bottom dwelling fish such as loaches and corys as they love to dig into the gravel for food.

Again this is personal taste but coloured gravels I think ruin the look of a planted aquarium. I believe a dark brown or even light brown colour highlights the plants and enhances the colours of the fish.

Nature has had a long time to perfect its systems so why mess with it.

Driftwood & Bogwood

These types of wood must be thoroughly cleaned and soaked in boiling water for a few days before they are ready for the aquarium.

Bogwood or Mopani wood is a great addition to any aquarium and is vital if you have plecos in your tank. They love to gnaw at the wood.

To prepare bogwood or Mopani wood you must first give it a scrub with hot water only.

Then once you have done that soak it in a bucket of boiling water for about 3 days.

You will need to replace the water every day until it is clear.

You can also attach some cool plants to your wood such as anubias or java fern.

Air Pumps

Little air pumps allow you to create some great looking effects with air stones and bubble walls.

All you need to get is an air pump, some silicone tubing, an airstone or bubble wall and a non-return valve to stop the water syphoning out your tank through the tubing.

The size of your pump depends on the size of your air stone or bubble wall. The columns you need to take note of is the size of your air wall and the air flow and get a pump with the appropriate airflow for the size of feature.

Model	Powers filters in aquariums up to approx.		Size of Airwall		Max no. of other features	Air Flow (L/hr)	Pressure (mbar)
AVMINI	46cm (18" long)	OR	1 x 1" Airstone	OR	1	75	0.22
AV1	60cm (24" long)	OR	1 x 12" Airwall	OR	2	170	0.23
AV2	100cm (36" long)	OR	1 x 18" Airwall	OR	4	200	0.27
AV3	120cm (48" long)	OR	4 x 12" Airwall	OR	6	2 x 250	0.23
AV4	150cm (60" long)	OR	4 x 18" Airwall	OR	8	2 x 300	0.23

These are manufacturer's recommendations and are usually exaggerated and if you want to run bubble walls or air stone ornaments some air pumps are rated for different sizes of tanks, but these ratings are, actually, nearly irrelevant to choosing the correct air pump.

For example, the AVMINI above will be sufficient for up to a 30cm air wall and the ornaments shown above.

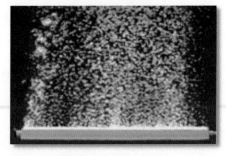

Tanks deeper than 50cm or much bigger ornaments might need more air flow, eg next model up. Check the air flow rating on the side of the ornaments/airwall you want to install.

You don't want to end up with too much air flow as it will create too powerful a bubble wall which is not good for some types of fish and will quickly deplete any CO_2 in planted tanks.

Bucket & Pump

Large bucket and pond pump. This will make it easier to prepare fresh water and pump it back into the aquarium. Pumps are only needed for large tanks. Smaller ones, a large watering can is handy to use.

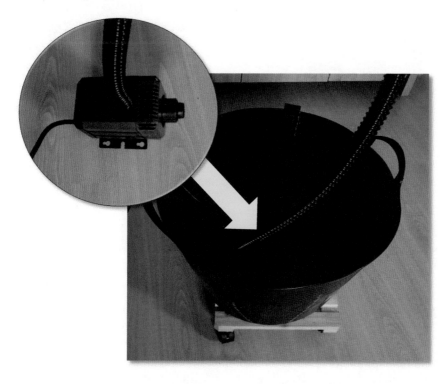

I used a pump like the one below. It should be fully submersible and rated at least 1400ltr/hour.

Other Tools

Long handle plant tweezers and cutters for trimming off leaves on live plants without having to put your hands and arms in the water

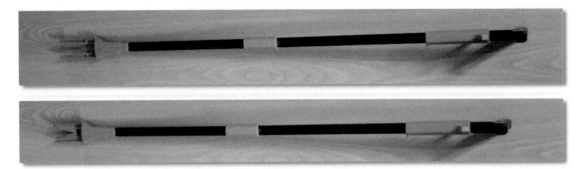

Fish nets. One with a long handle, makes handling fish a lot easier. Select the size of the net depending on the size of fish you get. For example the top net is ideal for guppies.

Something to keep the inside of the glass clean from algae

A magnetic algae cleaner or an algae sponge pad with a long pole handle to save you putting your hands in the tank.

These can be great for cleaning the inside of the glass, don't clean too far down as you will disturb all the substrate on the bottom.

Leave the bottom bits for a bristlenose plec.

Setting Up

Setup your Tank

Once you have your tank positioned on a stable cabinet in the place where you want it, begin to build the tank. Add your filter, install it according to the manufacturer's instructions. If it's an internal filter place it in the back right hand corner as shown below. This will give the best water circulation.

Next place the heater in the opposite back corner of the tank as shown below. Make sure your heater doesn't touch anything that will be going in the tank such as rocks or substrate. This can cause the glass on the heater to crack.

Install the lights in the hood according to the manufacturer's instructions. Do not turn anything on (except the lights) at this point. The heater & filter can only work under water.

Add the Planting Substrate & Gravel

Add your planting substrate & gravel to the bottom. Check the packaging – some gravel needs to be washed before use. Do not wash the bottom layer of planting substrate.

Bottom layer, either eco-complete, tetra or other planting substrate. Add enough for 2" deep

Top off with a layer of fine gravel. Use enough for about 1"

Level the substrate off into a nice bed.

Now is a good time to add all your rocks, caves, and any other décor according to taste.

Add your Rocks & Decor

Make sure you give them a good clean with hot water only before putting them in. Lay them nicely across the bed, making the best use of the space. Make sure you leave space behind and in between them for plants. Leave the front section for small items.

Fill the tank with water only to about 2 inches above the surface of the substrate, take care not to disturb the substrate too much. The idea of just filling the tank a couple of inches makes it easier to plant your plants. Working at arm's length in a tank full of water is more difficult.

This is now the best time to get your plants.

Plant your Plants

Some good examples of plants to start off with that are popular.

- Cryptocorynes, Echinodorus (sword plants),
- Egeria Densa (anacharis),
- Hornwort,
- Java Moss,
- Java Fern,
- Ludwigia,
- Rotalas,
- Water sprite,
- Hygrophilas (water wisteria and brethren),
- Marsilea sp (water clover).

See next section on getting plants & planting the aquarium

Once you have planted all your plants and got your tank looking nice, fill the tank to the maximum fill line.

Once it is full of water measure out the required amount of water conditioner and add it to the tank. Then fire up the filter and heater.

Check everything is working both heater and filter. Monitor the water temperature with a thermometer.

You are now ready to cycle your tank.

See next section on preparing the tank for fish a bit later in this book. Do not skip this step it's probably the most important step to building a healthy aquarium

Getting Plants

Some beautiful hardy plants to start off with

Anubias Nana

Quick Stats

Care Level: Easy
Lighting: Moderate
Placement: Foreground
Water Conditions: 22-27° C, KH 3-8, pH 6.0-7.5
Propagation: Rhizome Division
Max. Size: 15cm
Supplements: Substrate Fertilizer

Overview

Anubias nana is a hardy plant that is an aquarium favourite among many hobbyists. This rosette plant may reach up to 15cm in length and has beautiful dark green leaves in low, handsome clumps. They usually have diagonal lines running from the centre vein to the leaf perimeter.

Anubias nana has tall, variable foliage that is usually pointed to ovate. It prefers moderate lighting, an alkalinity of 3 - 8 dKH, and a pH of 6.0 - 7.5. When planting the aquatic plant, take special care of the rhizome and the roots. A quality substrate fertilizer is necessary as well as a warmed tank bottom. CO2 fertilization is also recommended.

Because it grows well from cuttings, you can usually reproduce it easily. Under correct water conditions, the Anubias nana propagates by side shoots on the rhizome, causing rhizome division.

It should be attached to logs in an aquarium to form lovely tropical scenes.

Java Fern

Care Level: Easy
Lighting: Low to Moderate
Placement: Mid-ground
Water Conditions: 20-27° C, KH 3-8, pH 6.0-7.5
Propagation: Rhizome Division, Adventitious Plants
Max. Size: 20cm
Supplements: High Quality Aquarium Fertilizer

Overview

Java Fern is a beautiful addition to the freshwater, planted aquarium. Growing around 20cm tall, with creeping, green rhizomes, Java Ferns are well suited for not only planted aquariums, but also those that contain cichlids and other large South American fish.

Java Ferns will do well if planted in moderate light as well as in a shaded area. It is amphibious, meaning that it will grow either partially or fully submersed. Provide at least 2 watts per gallon of light supplied by full spectrum (5000-7000K) bulbs.

Java Ferns will thrive in an aquarium with an alkalinity of 3-8 dKH and a pH of 6.0 to 7.5. They will propagate by adventitious plants on leaves & roots, and rhizome division may also be seen.

Java Fern looks great planted singly, or in groups if there is enough room in the aquarium. It should be attached to rocks or logs

Amazon Sword

Care Level: Moderate
Lighting: Moderate
Placement: Background
Water Conditions: 22-27° C, KH 3-8, pH 6.5-7.5
Propagation: Peduncles
Max. Size: 35cm
Color Form: Green
Supplements: Iron-Rich Fertilizer
Origin: Farm Raised, USA
Family: Alismataceae

Overview

The Amazon Sword Plant, is a Rosette plant that is very popular with aquarium hobbyists. They are capable of reaching approximately half a metre in height under proper water conditions. The Amazon Sword Plant has short rhizomes, numerous lance shaped leaves that are pale to dark green with sharply pointed tips, and fairly short stems. It is an amphibious plant that will grow either partially or fully submersed.

For the most beautiful Amazon Sword Plants, a loose substrate and an iron-rich fertilizer must be used. The Amazon Sword Plant requires at least 2 watts per gallon of full spectrum lighting (5000-7000K).

Best cultivated in large aquariums, Amazon Sword Plants make a great focal point if used singly. When used in groups, they create an interesting background when grown with other aquarium plants.

Planting the Aquarium

Place taller plants at the back such as amazon sword and shorter plants at the front such as anubias nana or wheat plant.

Arrange your larger plants across the back and sides taking care not to block the filter. This will provide ample swimming space across the centre front of the tank. Smaller plants at the front.

Try combining plants with different leaf shapes and shades – dark green, light green etc

Make sure you plant them in groups rather than dotting individual plants around the tank and allow room to grow.

Carefully remove the plant from its little pot and take all the rock wool from around the roots. Also check in there for snails.

Plant the roots about an inch into the substrate, take care not to bury too much of the stems (or crown) as it may rot. Just bury the roots.

Depending on the type of plant, sometimes it is useful to weight them down with lead weights.

These are readily available in most aquarium stores and should be loosely wrapped around the plant as not to choke it or break the roots as it grows.

For anubias nana and java fern, it is best to attach these to a rock, tank ornament or a piece of driftwood as they tend to rot if planted in the substrate.

You may need to tie the plant on at first with a piece of nylon thread or fine fishing line until the roots get a hold for themselves.

Prepare the Tank for Fish

Nitrogen Cycle

The nitrogen cycle is the process whereby ammonia secreted by animals as waste, is converted by bacteria to nitrite and then into nitrate.

Note the spellings: nitrite is the toxic one. Nitrate is far less toxic

Ammonia and nitrite are highly toxic to fish in very low concentrations, so establishing the bacteria colonies that quickly convert these compounds to nitrate is crucial to creating a healthy environment for fish.

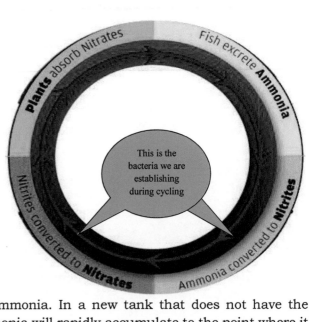

Nitrate are far less toxic, and can easily be removed through periodic water changes or consumption by live plants.

Most fish mortality in new tanks can be traced to the lack of an established nitrogen cycle in the tank.

Fish excrete urea, which contains ammonia. In a new tank that does not have the necessary bacteria colonies, this ammonia will rapidly accumulate to the point where it is toxic to the fish.

Depending on the size of the tank and the number of fish, the ammonia may become toxic within one day to a week.

When a new tank is setup there is no bacteria established to convert ammonia to nitrites and then to nitrates as explained above.

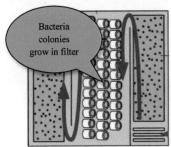

Cycling is the process of establishing the bacteria colonies which will mostly locate in the filter media but will also coat all the walls, rocks in the aquarium. The bacteria will also grow in the substrate, this is why it's important to have a good quality substrate as the bacteria colonies will grow and help consume toxins from fish waste and uneaten food that falls to the floor of the tank.

This is the secret to maintaining a healthy clean fish tank.

Cycling the Tank

All it takes to some kind of an ammonia source. Pure ammonia available in most home improvement stores or Garden shops and is sometimes labelled as ammonium hydroxide. If using this option, make sure the ammonia is free of any surfactants, dyes or perfumes as they may poison the fish in long term.

To test for surfactants, just shake the ammonia bottle before purchasing and if it fizzles or gives bubbles then there are surfactants present. Also use only pure ammonia — that is one which is not scented.

To start the cycling, add ammonia to the tank, depending on the concentration of your pure ammonia (it will tell you on the side of the bottle, and is usually somewhere around 9.5%).

To get your tank concentration to 5ppm, a 50litre tank would need about 2.5ml

My tank is 250litre so I added about 14ml

Test the water every 24 hours and wait to see the ammonia reading drop. At this point the filter contains bacteria that break down ammonia into nitrite, so the cycle has started.

 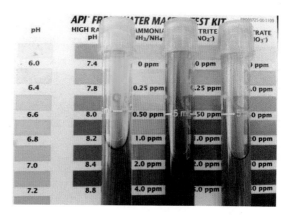

Keeping a cycling diary is recommended so you can plot the changes/patterns emerging.

Add more ammonia (about 5ml) to raise the level in the tank back up to the level you chose to start with. Keep testing for ammonia every 24 hours and now test for nitrite too.

Wait until the nitrite level starts to drop, (they will be sky high for a few weeks) continuing to add ammonia to feed the bacteria in the tank. Nitrite is often the most annoying reading as once it drops it will linger at low levels until sometimes just a few days before the end of the full cycle.

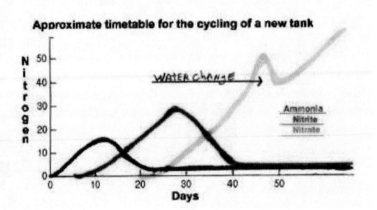

When you have 0ppm of ammonia, 0 ppm of nitrite, and a nitrate reading, your tank is ready for fish.

Continue adding ammonia until you add your fish. This will keep the bacteria from dying.

Before adding fish, do a large water change (70-90%) to get your nitrate under 40ppm.

Once the fish are added, continue to test the water for both ammonia and nitrite to ensure that no spikes occur.

Do not add any ammonia once fish are added.

Here is a reference guide to help you read the api test. The information below will help you gauge where your levels should be as well as understand the results.

pH– NORMAL RANGE: 6.5-8.2 This is the measure of acidity or alkalinity of the water. Rapid changes in pH are detrimental to fish.

Chlorine and Chloramine – NORMAL RESULTS: 0.0 mg/L This is added to city water supplies to make the water supply safe for human consumption. Be certain to always use a water conditioner when adding water to an aquarium because any amount of chlorine is toxic to fish.

Ammonia – NORMAL RESULTS: 0.0-0.25 mg/L Aquariums with properly operating filtration systems should have no ammonia present (after they have been cycled). In new aquariums, Ammonia Removers can be used to lower ammonia levels, along with partial water changes.

Nitrite – NORMAL RESULTS: 0.0-0.05 mg/L Nitrite reduces the ability of the fish's blood to carry oxygen. You can remove excess nitrite from an aquarium by performing a partial water change.

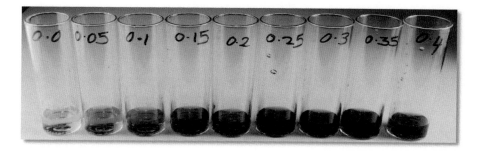

Nitrate – NORMAL RANGE: 0-40 mg/L If nitrate levels exceed 40 mg/L, water changes can be used to lower the concentration. High levels of nitrate can also cause increased algae growth.

Hardness – NORMAL RANGE: 100-250 mg/L Water with high hardness usually has a high pH. Softening the water will lower the pH. Most fish will adapt to moderate hardness levels.

Alkalinity – NORMAL RANGE: 120-300 mg/L With low alkalinity water, your aquarium may experience sudden and deadly pH shifts. Increase the alkalinity of the water to stabilize the pH.

Temperature – NORMAL RANGE: 74-82° F (23-28° C) Use an aquarium heater to maintain stable water temperatures. Rapid temperature changes are harmful to tropical fish.

Getting Fish

Great fish to start off with. Some are more hardy than others and should only be introduced to an established aquarium. Loaches require pristine water conditions to thrive.

In this section I have included some great starter fish to get in your tank and also some of the fish that have given me much pleasure over the years.

How many fish can I get? Below is a rough summary of the stocking levels.

Capacity	Aquarium Dimensions W x D x H	Cabinet Dimensions W x D x H	Fish Stocking Level	
			Tropical	Coldwater
232 L (60 U.S. gal.)	85 x 48 x 65 cm (33" x 18.75" x 25.5")	85 x 48 x 68 cm (33" x 18.75" x 26.75")	116 cm (46")	77 cm (30")
275 L (72 U.S. gal.)	100 x 48 x 65 cm (39" x 18.75" x 25.5")	100 x 48 x 68 cm (39" x 18.75" x 26.75")	120 cm (47")	80 cm (31.5")
323 L (85 U.S. gal.)	120 x 48 x 65 cm (47" x 18.75" x 25.5")	120 x 48 x 68 cm (47" x 18.75" x 26.75")	140 cm (55")	90 cm (35")
500 L (130 U.S. gal.)	150 x 58 x 65 cm (60 x 22.8 x 25.5)	150 x 58 x 68 cm (60 x 22.8 x 26.75 cm)	250 cm (98")	166 cm (65")

For example you should allow about 1 or 2 litres of water for each cm of tropical fish.

So for a 60 litre tank, I can add 60cms of fish

Now say I want to keep guppies. Guppies are about 6cm from their nose to the base of their tail

$60 \div 6 = 10$

So as a rough guide I could keep 10, 6cm fish in a 60 litre tank

Remember this is only a rough guide and you should also take into account the species and size of the fish and the size of the filters you have in your tank because you wouldn't be able to keep a 20-30cm loach in a 60litre tank even though you have 60cms of potential fish space.

Guppy

Quick Stats

Scientific Name(s): Poecilia reticulata
Difficulty: Easy
Maximum Size: 6cms
Minimum Tank Volume: 65 litres
Water Temperature Range: 23-28°C

Overview

A fantastic beginner fish, tolerant of a wide range of water parameters and entertaining to watch

Peaceful. Will happily co-exist with similar sized fish, but fin-nippers should be avoided as the elaborate fins of the males make tempting targets.

A good base of quality flake supplemented with twice weekly treats of bloodworm, daphnia and brine shrimp will ensure these fish maintain their elaborate colours and active nature.

Should be kept in groups of no less than 6 as these are shoaling fish. Females should outnumber males at least 2 to 1.

Molly

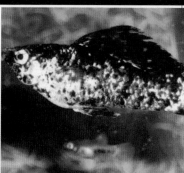

Scientific Name(s): Poecilia sphenops
Difficulty: Easy
Maximum Size: 15cms
Minimum Tank Volume: 60 litres
Water Temperature Range: 25-28°C

Overview

Very entertaining to young children and adults alike, they are cheeky and alert.

Mollies will eat anything, but their natural diet is largely herbivorous with a jaw and digestive tract designed for efficient scraping and grazing of algae and digestion of low protein vegetable matter. Their diet should be based around algae wafers, vegetarian flake and fresh veg.

Platy

Quick Stats

Scientific Name(s): Xiphophorus maculatus
Difficulty: Easy
Maximum Size: 7cms
Minimum Tank Volume: 60 litres
Water Temperature Range: 20-26°C

Overview

Peaceful community fish. Excellent beginner's fish for more alkaline water. Exhibits no aggression, even between males. Best kept in a well planted tank as 2 male per 2-3 females to prevent any one female being harassed.

Unfussy and will take most foods offered.

Compatible with other peaceful community fish.

Tetras

Rummy Nose

Quick Stats	
	**Difficulty:** Easy **Maximum Size:** 5cm **Minimum Tank Size:** 40 litre **Water Temperature Range:** 22-25° C

Overview

The True Rummy-Nose Tetra gets its name from the red blushing across its nose and face. It has a mirror-like silver body and a jet-black tail striped with white.

The True Rummy-Nose Tetra is a peaceful omnivore that makes an excellent addition to community aquariums with non-aggressive tank mates.

In addition to plants, decorate the aquarium with scattered rocks and driftwood to simulate its natural habitat.

A school of six or more Rummy Nose Tetras creates an impressive aquarium display. For best care, offer a variety of foods, including brine shrimp or daphnia, freeze-dried bloodworms and tubifex, micro pellet food, and high quality flake diets.

Corys

Panda

Quick Stats

Scientific Name(s): Corydoras panda
Difficulty: Easy
Maximum Size: 5cm
Minimum Tank Volume: 60 litres
Water Temperature Range: 20-25°C

Overview

A small Cory and a popular choice for community aquaria, cute little things. They like a lot of hiding places.

Omnivorous. This species is an excellent scavenger that will work to keep the aquarium substrate clean of excess foodstuffs and some decaying plant matter. Supplemental foods such as bloodworms, tubifex, flake food, or sinking carnivore pellets should be offered to ensure proper nutrition

Keep in a group of at least 6 or more in a tank with fine substrate.

Compatible with most similar sized community fish.

Peppered Cory

Scientific Name(s): Corydoras palaetus
Difficulty: Easy
Maximum Size: 7cms
Minimum Tank Volume: 60 litres
Water Temperature Range: 20-26°C

Overview

A medium sized Cory and a popular choice for community aquaria. They like a lot of hiding places.

Omnivorous. Takes pellets, algae wafers and frozen and live food. They also love peas and other cooked vegetables.

Keep in a group of at least 6 or more in a tank with fine substrate.

Compatible with most similar sized community fish.

Bronze Cory

Scientific Name(s): Corydoras aeneus
Difficulty: Easy
Maximum Size: 7.5cm
Minimum Tank Volume: 90 litre
Water Temperature Range: 25°C - 28°C

Overview

These are peaceful scavengers - in the wild they eat small insects, worms, crustaceans and plant matter. Use a good sinking pellet food and they will also eat left over flakes, algae wafers, shrimp pellets, etc

Keep in a group of at least 6 or more in a tank with fine substrate.

Compatible with most similar sized community fish

Plecos

Bristlenose

Scientific Name(s): Ancistrus sp.
Difficulty: Easy
Maximum Size: 15cms
Minimum Tank Volume: 90 litres
Water Temperature Range: 22-27°C

Overview

Provide good cover/caves of bogwood, stones, rocks etc

They love to eat and will feed on algae although this is insufficient to properly feed them. They should also have cucumber, courgette/zucchini, lettuce, spinach, boiled potatoes and shelled peas and algae wafers/sinking pellets. As a result they have a large bioload and produce a lot of waste so make sure you have a good filter. They also must have some bogwood or driftwood as this aids their digestion.

They are very peaceful and solitary

Loaches

Clown Loach

Quick Stats

Scientific Name(s): Chromobotia macracanthus
Difficulty: medium to difficult
Maximum Size: 40cms
Minimum Tank Volume: 300-500 litres
Water Temperature Range: 25-30°C

Overview

This is a wonderful, large, social, shoaling fish and should only be kept in large aquariums in a group of at least 5. Never in pairs or alone.

They are constantly hungry and will readily accept most flake, frozen foods. Vegetables and fruits are also taken. Eats most invertebrates, loves wormy foods and can even be hand fed. They will nibble on softer leaved plants.

Keep in a well planted tank with subdued lighting and plenty of hiding places as they can be a shy species. Use a small rounded fine gravel or a sand substrate, avoid abrasive substrates that will damage their barbels.

Polkadot Loach

Quick Stats

Scientific Name(s): Botia kubotai
Difficulty: Medium
Maximum Size: 13cm
Minimum Tank Volume: 100litre
Water Temperature Range: 24-28°C

Overview

A very graceful, social fish, it is best kept in groups of three or more. Caves and hiding places should be provided giving them greater security and generally makes them bolder.

Like most bottom-dwellers the substrate should consist of a fine-grained or round-edged gravel.

Omnivorous; will readily take both commercially prepared foods and frozen foods, they love a bit of cucumber too. Also a good snail eater.

YoYo Loach

Scientific Name(s): Botia almorhae, Botia lochata
Difficulty: Medium
Maximum Size: 15cms
Minimum Tank Volume: 150 litres
Water Temperature Range: 20-28°C

Overview

Generally peaceful loach with similar social structure and behavior and should be kept in a group of at least 5

They like plenty of hiding places, bogwood, rocks, caves etc with a sandy or fine substrate preferred to avoid barbel damage when searching for food.

Good snail eater

Chain Loach

Quick Stats

Scientific Name(s): Ambastaia sidthimunki
Difficulty: Medium
Maximum Size: 6cms
Minimum Tank Volume: 60 litres
Water Temperature Range: 24-28°C

Overview

These little loaches are best kept in large groups, and 5 really is considered the absolute minimum.

The aquarium should have a fine soft sandy substrate in order to protect their delicate barbels, and should be furnished with bogwood, rocky caves and aquatic plants.

Pristine water quality with a moderate amount of flow should be provided.

They will accept most small foods offered. Sinking catfish pellets, micro pellets, flake, algae wafers. Also a good snail eater.

Adding Fish to your Tank

Turn off aquarium lights and dim the lights in the room where the shipping box will be opened. Never open the box in bright light - severe stress or trauma may result from sudden exposure to bright light.

Float the sealed bag in the aquarium for 15 minutes without opening it. This step allows the water in the bag to adjust slowly to the temperature of the aquarium, while maintaining a high level of dissolved oxygen.

After floating the sealed bag for 15 minutes, cut it open just under the knot or clip and roll open the top of the bag down to create an air pocket within the lip of the bag as shown below.

This will enable the bag to float on the surface of the water.

Gently add 1/2 cup of your aquarium water to the bag.

Repeat every ten minutes for about half an hour to an hour. This is to slowly adjust the water chemistry in the bag to match the water in your tank so it is not so much of a shock to the fish. It's like us quickly going from a hot room to the freezing cold outside in a t-shirt.

Gently net your fish from the bag and him release into the aquarium. Be patient and gentle, the fish will be stressed at this point and will try to escape.

Remove the bag from the aquarium. Keep the water handy just in case there is a problem with your fish. Do not release shipping water directly into the aquarium.

Dose the aquarium with 5ml of stress coat.

If your fish has settled in then discard the water.

Feeding Time

This is one of my favourite parts, watching the fish feed and feeding them by hand

Loaches tucking into cucumber salad

Bristlenose enjoying her lunch

Hungry loaches gobble a spot of algae wafer

Panda cory enjoying some pellets

I get a lot of enjoyment hand feeding loaches and the other fish. If you use your hands always make sure they are clean and free from hand cream, soaps etc as these can poison the fish.

Get yourself a good set of feeding tongs and use them to dip the food below the surface and watch them feed. The fish love it and by doing it this way the fish become very tame and interact with you more.

As soon as they see you, they start to gather at the top of the aquarium waiting for their food.

The fish's staple diet usually consists of some kind of flake or pellet food. Floating flakes are ideal for fish that swim near the top of middle of the aquarium, although bottom dwellers like loaches and corys might get whatever falls to the floor.

For bottom dwellers such as corys and loaches a sinking pellet food would be more suitable for them as it sinks to the bottom allowing these fish to feed naturally from the floor of the tank. Some pellets can be a bit large for the smaller of the bottom dwellers such as panda corys so you may need to help them out and crush the pellets lightly to make them easier to eat

Another good type of food is an algae wafer. These are also great for bottom dwellers but are especially good for plecos such as bristlenose. Depending on the size of your plec again you might have to break bits off the algae wafer to feed them as they may not be able to eat a full one and any leftover food will rot.

How much should you feed your fish? This is a difficult question to answer as different fish have different requirements. The rule of thumb is to feed them all they can eat in a couple of minutes. So I would add a few flakes at a time and see if they eat it all, then add a bit more. You don't want any uneaten food left behind as it will rot.

You may need to add a mixture of food, eg, flakes for top feeders mixed with pellets or chips for bottom feeders so the flakes keep the top feeders busy giving the pellets time to drop to the floor for the bottom feeders otherwise the more dominant fish will eat anything they can find leaving none for the bottom feeders.

Make sure all the fish receive some.

By doing it this way you will soon get to know the fish's feeding habits and you will be able to gauge how much to feed them without leaving them underfed or leftover food in the tank.

On the left are some chips suitable for bottom feeders.

Here is a summary of the different types of food on the market and what type of fish they are suitable for.

Food Format	Water Level	Best For	Notes
Flakes	Floating	Top Feeders	Shortest retention of full vitamin and nutritional content. Replace every month.
Pellets or Sticks	Either sinking or floating	Sinking are good for mid-water feeders; floating good for top feeders	Usually larger; for larger fish
Granules	Either sinking or floating	Sinking are good for mid-water feeders; floating good for top feeders	Essentially smaller pellets
Wafers/Tablets	Sinking	Bottom-feeders and scavengers	Usually made to meet nutrient needs of bottom-feeders

Fish can be carnivorous meaning they eat fish based foods, insects or smaller fish. They can be herbivorous meaning they eat plants, algae, seaweed etc. They can also be omnivorous meaning they eat both types of food. This should be taken into account when buying food for your fish. It's always worth finding out which of the three categories they fall into then buy your food accordingly. Below is a summary of the different diet types.

Diet Type	Restrictions	Popular Example	Natural Diet	Staple Needs (Daily)
Carnivore	Derive no/minimal nutrients from vegetation	Bettas, Discus, Anthias	Smaller fish, invertebrates, crustaceans, insects	Fish-protein based (fish meals, squid meals, shrimp, krill)
Herbivore	Cannot digest meats or most land plants	Otos & Plecos (catfish), some African cichlids, tangs	Live plants, seaweed, algae	Plant-protein based - spirulina, algae, soybean meal
Omnivore	Cannot digest some grains and plants (look for aquatic plants)	Goldfish, Gouramis, Clownfish	A variety of animal and vegetative matter	Balance of meat & plant proteins (a good tropical or marine staple)

Tank Maintenance

Water Changes

Once a week switch off your heater then syphon out 20% of the volume of water in your tank into a bucket.

   Eg: My tank is 250 litre so 20% is about 40-50 litres.

At the same time with the head of your syphon use it to vacuum up all the muck from the bottom. This will help keep your water pure.

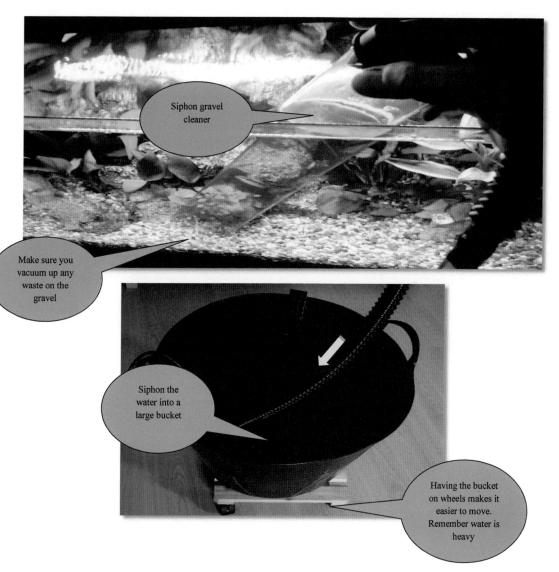

Siphon gravel cleaner

Make sure you vacuum up any waste on the gravel

Siphon the water into a large bucket

Having the bucket on wheels makes it easier to move. Remember water is heavy

Cleaning your Filter

Over time the sponges inside your filter will clog and this is what needs to be cleaned out regularly. I would clean it about once a month

In this cleaning guide I use a Fluval 306 but the principles can be applied to cleaning any filter.

It is a good idea to clean your filter during a water change as you will have a bucket of tank water to use.

Unhooking the Filter

If your filter allows for it block off the hoses to maintain water vacuum in the hoses. For the Fluval series of canister filters this is achieved by pulling up the grey lever on the hose attachment.

If your filter does not have this capability you might need to withdraw the filter intake from the tank otherwise your intake will draw water upon disconnection from the canister unit.

Once the hose is blocked off or the intake has been removed from the tank it is then safe to turn off power to the canister unit. Once this is done disconnect the hoses (or hose unit if you're using a Fluval) from the unit and carry the filter to the workspace.

Cleaning the Sponges

Set it down on a workspace open up the filter (for Fluvals this is done by lifting the two light grey clamps on either side of the unit) and have a look inside, it should look mucky like this:

First clean the sponge media as it is easily the dirtiest component of a canister filter. With the Fluval models the sponge media is attached to a tray unit. To access the media simply lift the unit as shown above

Most manuals and fish shops recommend throwing out this media and replacing it with new media, the reason for this is money is made when you are continually buying new media. Do not do this, your tank will benefit from keeping the old media as it will contain all the necessary bacteria to remove toxins from the water.

It is **IMPORTANT NEVER to use TAP WATER** to clean filter components as chlorine/chloramine in the tap water will destroy your biological bacteria and render your filter useless upon reconnection.

Using your syphon fill a bucket with tank water from the aquarium and use this to rinse off the sponge media. The bucket water will get dirty fast so use additional tank water as required.

Wring the sponges out in the tank water till it is clean. Just do it enough to get rid of all the solid waste and gunk.

Once all mechanical media is cleaned leave it in some tank water do not allow it to dry out.

Rinse out the Biological Media or Ceramic Rings

In the Fluval 06 filters with the sponge media sometimes the biological filter baskets do get a decent amount of muck in them.

I would only clean the biological filter baskets if it is clogged, blocked or looks really dirty, otherwise leave it alone as you do not want to disturb the bacterial colonies that grow on the rings. This is responsible for removing the toxins from the water such as ammonia.

To clean them out gently rinse them by moving the basket up and down a few times in a bucket of tank water just enough so the solid waste falls out. There is no need to remove all the chips. I use the same bucket of water for all three stacks of baskets. Once rinsed simply set aside the biological media. Do not allow to dry out.

Clean the Filter Housing & Impeller Unit

Empty out the dirty water from inside the canister housing and give it a scrub with your filter sponge. It is ok for the inside of the housing to feel slimy but remove any solid build up.

The impeller unit can be prone to heavy clogging because water flow is at its strongest here. On most canister filters the impeller area can be a bit fiddly to clean so this is where the old toothbrush comes in handy.

Be especially gentle with the propeller shaft as they are prone to breaking and are usually expensive to replace for what is essentially a ceramic rod.

Put it back together

Once everything is clean and reassembled it should look something like this:

The secret to clear water is not to actually clean the filter thoroughly just to remove gunk and solid waste but retaining the bacterial colonies to purify the water.

Before attaching the propeller unit be sure to line the rubber seal with vaseline. This prolongs the life of the seal and stops it from getting brittle over time.

After it's all assembled carry the filter unit back to the tank.

Restarting the filter

Before restarting the filter grab a clean kitchen sponge (not one that has been used for washing up as it will have soap and detergent that will poison the fish). I would keep one spare just for fish tank maintenance.

When the hoses are left for a while without a constant water flow through them gunk starts to fall off the insides and if not caught in a sponge will make your tank look horrible for a few hours after filter restart.

With the sponge over the output it's now time to prime the filter. For the Fluvals this is simply a matter of clipping the hose unit back onto the top of the filter and then pushing the black lever down. You might have to pump the manual primer a few times to get it going and then water should flow until the canister is full.

For other brands the concept is the same, reconnect the hoses and prime the unit till it is full of water.

Once water stops flowing into the unit it's time to turn the filter back on. Plug in the unit and watch the outflow, water should start pouring from the sponge otherwise you might have to try a few plug/unplugs till it gets going.

One trick I've learnt with the Fluvals is that if you pump the primer heavily a few times and plug in the unit whilst doing this it gets it going pretty easily.

Let the flow run for a few minutes and then carefully remove the sponge from the output hose being careful not to let the gunk captured escape into the tank.

Maintaining Plants

Now is a good time to do any maintenance on your plants while the water level is lower during a water chance. This makes it easier to work in the water.

Inspect your plants for any dead or dying leaves and trim them off as near to the base as possible with your long handled cutters. Don't leave any storks with no leaves as they will just rot in the tank.

Also cut back any leaves that are growing too big etc.

Dose with a good liquid plant fertiliser if required.

If your plants are not growing particularly well and you have sufficient light and fertilisers, then it could be due to lack of CO_2 in the water. There are a number of ways to add CO_2 and plenty of devices on the market to choose from but you can make your own CO_2 reactor.

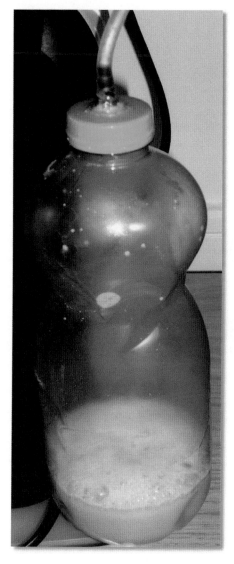

Get yourself a litre plastic drinks bottle or soda bottle and glue a piece of silicon tubing to the cap. Best glue to use is a hot melt glue gun as it makes a non-toxic seal.

Connect the other end to the filter head in the aquarium so the bubbles gently flow into the water with the current.

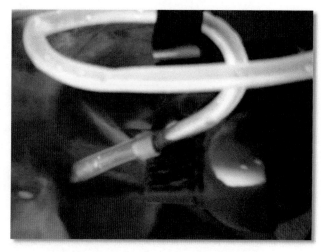

Fill the bottle with a teaspoon of yeast and a couple of teaspoons of sugar. Then fill the bottle about 2 inches from the bottom with warm water (not boiling or hot). Put the cap on tightly and mix it around.

After a few minutes the yeast begin to convert the sugar and will start to release CO_2 into the water.

Keep an eye on your fish as too much CO_2 can cause them to become listless or even poison them.

Don't let any of that gunge at the bottom of the bottle get in the pipes or into the aquarium as it will contain alcohol and poison the fish.

Only use this when the aquarium lights are on. Don't run it when the lights are off. Plants only require CO_2 when there is light.

Preparing Fresh Water

Fill your bucket with the same amount fresh water as you took out the tank.

Remember this water is probably cold so you need to get it up to the same temperature as the water in your tank. You can do this by adding a couple of boiled kettles of water just enough to raise the temperature of the water in the bucket. Aim for about 25°C. A small mercury thermometer is handy to use here.

Once the temperature of the water is correct, add a dose of water conditioner (I use API Stress Coat) to the water in the bucket and stir. Let it stand for a few minutes.

Refilling the Tank

Now the bucket is going to be heavy so to save you from having to lift the bucket and pour it into the tank, put your submersible pump in the bucket and hook the outlet pipe over the side of the tank.

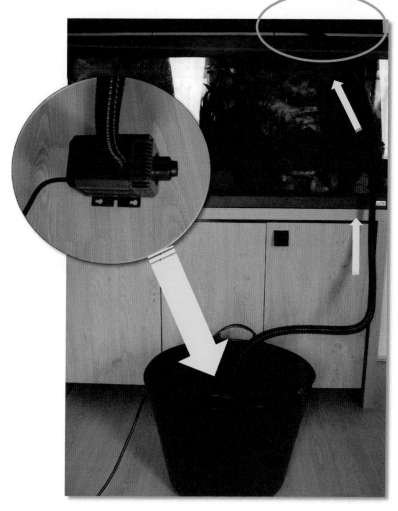

Turn on your pump and watch the water flow back into the tank. Make sure you stop the pump when the water runs out or you reach the max fill line on the tank.

For smaller tanks under 100litres try using a large watering can to prepare your water and refill the tank.

Common Problems

Water Quality

If your fish are displaying symptoms such as, not eating, rapid gill movement, staying near surface, listless at bottom of tank or erratic movements, these symptoms can usually be traced back to water quality problems, such as high ammonia or high nitrite levels.

What to do if Ammonia/Nitrite levels are high

Immediately carry out a water change, up to 40% if necessary and prepare fresh conditioned water for your fish.

Check the filter to make sure it isn't blocked and make sure the filter flow is circulating around the tank.

Algae

A lot of algae can be caused by high amount of phosphate and nitrate in the water. Phosphate is present in tap water and also in some kinds of fish foods.

Brown algae is usually caused by low light and green algae is caused by direct sunlight or too much light.

Try some phosphate remover or get yourself a bristlenose plec if your tank is big enough. Also try an algae magnet to clean the glass.

Plants

Poor colour, leaves falling off or yellow spots on the leaves can be due to a lack of iron. This can happen after a few months of planting as the plants deplete the nutrients in the planting substrate. A good liquid fertilizer will help solve the problem.

Can also be due to lack of CO_2 and light.

Common Disease

Maintaining a clean tank, with regular water changes and maintenance to achieve crystal clear water with 0 ammonia and 0 nitrite is the best preventative precaution to your fish getting sick. However if they do get sick the infections are usually bacterial, fungal or parasitic.

Bacterial Infections: Inactivity, loss of colour, frayed fins, bloated body, cloudy eyes, open sores, abscesses, red streaks throughout body, reddening or inflammation of the skin, fins or internal organs, bulging eyes, difficulty breathing.

Fungal Infections (often secondary to another type of illness): Erratic swimming, darting, scratching, visible cotton-like tufts on skin, eyes, or mouth.

Parasitic Infections: Inactivity, loss of appetite, excess mucus or film on body, visible spots or worms, rapid breathing, scratching.

Here are some symptoms of some of the more common diseases. Please note that this is a guide and you should read all the labels on the medication to make sure it is treating the correct disease and to make sure that the medication is applied correctly and in the correct dose. Incorrectly used medication can be lethal to your fish.

Symptoms	Possible Diagnosis	Treatment
Greyish-white film on skin, damaged fins, ulcers, yellow to grey patches on gills, tissue on head may be eaten away.	Columnaris (Cotton Wool Disease)	Must be treated immediately with Over-the-counter antibiotic medications. Very contagious disinfect tank, rocks, net, etc.
Swelling of head, bulging eyes.	Corneybacteriosis	OTC antibiotics such as penicillin and tetracycline.
Swelling of abdomen, raised scales around swollen area.	Dropsy (Malawi Bloat) may be caused by internal bacterial infection (if swelling is sudden), parasites, or cancer (if swelling is gradual).	Add 1/8 teaspoon of Epsom salt for every 5 gallons of water and monitor for two weeks. Check for signs of bacterial infection or parasites for further treatment.
Ragged or decaying fins.	Fin rot	Check pH and correct as needed. If level is normal, use OTC antibiotic for fin or tail rot.
Erratic swimming, bloating or swelling in body, black patches on body or fins.	Myxobacteriosis -- rare	Medications, if any, are difficult to come by. Keep up on water maintenance to prevent it.
White or grey fungus on eyes.	Cataracts	OTC medication for fungus.
White or grey patches resembling cotton, excess mucus.	Mouth or Body Fungus	OTC medication for fungus. Usually added to water, but may need direct application.
White cotton-like patches on fins, body, or mouth.	True Fungus (Saprolegnia)	OTC medication for fungus. Check for symptoms of other illnesses.
Small string-like worms visible on fish, or burrowed in skin.	Anchor Worm	Over-the-counter medication for parasites.
Weight loss, strained breathing.	Copepods	OTC medication for parasites, also fungal treatment for possible secondary infection on damaged gills
White film, reddened areas on body, abnormal swimming, scratching, folded fins.	Costia (Slime Disease)	Must be treated quickly. Raise water temperature and use OTC medication for parasites. Salt treatment may work, as well.
Sluggishness, flashing, spider web lesions on skin, colour loss, reddened fins, drooping fins, fin damage.	Skin Flukes (Gyrodactylus)	OTC medication for parasites
Lack of appetite, weight loss, small holes or eroding pits appearing in the head.	Hole in Head Disease (Hexamita) more common in cichlids	OTC medication for Hole in Head Disease.

70

Scratching, white salt-like spots starting on head and spreading over whole body, rapid breathing, and cloudiness on eyes or fins.	Ich (Ichtyophthirius) very common	OTC medication for Ich or Ick.
Scratching, small worms hanging from body.	Leech	Salt treatment or OTC medication for parasites.
Erratic swimming, weight loss, loss of colour.	Neon Tetra Disease mostly affects tetras, danios, and barbs	Treatment is difficult look for a medication that treats gram-negative bacteria or with nalidixic acid as the active ingredient.
Darting, scratching, small yellow to white spots dusting skin.	Oodinium	OTC treatment for parasites.
Cloudy appearance on skin, red patches on skin where parasite has bitten.	Trichodina -- predominately freshwater	Salt treatment.
Red or bloody gills, gasping for air.	Ammonia Poisoning	No treatment. Regular water testing and maintenance will prevent it.
Small dark spots on fins and body.	Black Spot	OTC medication for parasites. Spots (cysts) may remain after treatment.
Cloudy white appearance to one or both eyes.	Cloudy Eye	Check for symptoms of another illness like velvet, ich, or tuberculosis. Treat with OTC medication.
String of faeces hanging from fish, swollen abdomen, sluggishness, disinterest in food, off-balance swimming.	Constipation	Stop feeding for 2-3 days and continue with a more varied diet including live and plant-based foods.
Small white spots that get larger over time possibly with black streaks.	Fish Pox	No treatment. Keep up on water maintenance and symptoms should cease after about 10-12 weeks.
Reddening on or under skin, sudden abnormal behaviour.	Inflammation	OTC antibiotic treatment.
Unusual bulging of one or both eyes.	Pop-eye (Exophthalmia)	OTC medication for bacterial infections and/or parasites. Check for other symptoms of bacterial or parasitic infections.
Fish struggles to swim, may float with head tipped down, or have difficulty surfacing, no balance, etc. May occur after eating.	Swim Bladder Disease	Stop feeding for 3-4 days. If symptoms persist, feed the affected fish a small amount of fresh spinach or a green pea without the skin (laxatives).
Swelling or distention for internal tumours, external can be seen growing on skin.	Tumours	Usually incurable. Consult a veterinarian about potassium iodide treatment for thyroid tumours.

Sluggishness, lack of appetite, open sores with red edges, possible fin rot.	Ulcers	OTC medication for bacterial infections.
Scratching, small gold to white spots, loss of colour, weight loss, difficulty breathing due to gill damage.	Velvet (Gold Dust Disease)	OTC medication for parasites

Treating Sick Fish

When you need to treat any fish, remove them from the main aquarium and place them in a little hospital tank about 15 litres with a small heater and filter.

From your aquarium store find the appropriate medication for the disease, some common ones are described above and add the medication to the hospital tank.

This is to prevent the medications from upsetting the biological balance in the main aquarium

Depending on the illness you may need to treat the main tank to prevent it from spreading to other fish.

Useful Unit Conversions

Some useful conversion charts to help you convert between the different units you are familiar with.

Inch to Cm		°C to °F		Litre to Gallon		Litre to Gallon	
0	0.00	10,0	50,0	51	13.4727746	76	20.07707588
1	2.54	11,0	51,8	52	13.73694665	77	20.34124793
2	5.08	12,0	53,6	53	14.0011187	78	20.60541998
3	7.62	13,0	55,4	54	14.26529075	79	20.86959203
4	10.16	14,0	57,2	55	14.52946281	80	21.13376408
5	12.70	15,0	59,0	56	14.79363486	81	21.39793613
6	15.24	16,0	60,8	57	15.05780691	82	21.66210818
7	17.78	17,0	62,6	58	15.32197896	83	21.92628023
8	20.32	18,0	64,4	59	15.58615101	84	22.19045228
9	22.86	19,0	66,2	60	15.85032306	85	22.45462434
10	25.40	20,0	68,0	61	16.11449511	86	22.71879639
11	27.94	21,0	69,8	62	16.37866716	87	22.98296844
12	30.48	22,0	71,6	63	16.64283921	88	23.24714049
13	33.02	23,0	73,4	64	16.90701126	89	23.51131254
14	35.56	24,0	75,2	65	17.17118332	90	23.77548459
15	38.10	25,0	77,0	66	17.43535537	100	26.4172051
16	40.64	26,0	78,8	67	17.69952742	125	33.02150638
17	43.18	27,0	80,6	68	17.96369947	150	39.62580765
18	45.72	28,0	82,4	69	18.22787152	175	46.23010893
19	48.26	29,0	84,2	70	18.49204357	200	52.8344102
20	50.80	30,0	86,0	71	18.75621562	250	66.04301275
21	53.34	31,0	87,8	72	19.02038767	300	79.2516153
22	55.88	32,0	89,6	73	19.28455972	500	132.0860255
23	58.42	33,0	91,4	74	19.54873177	750	198.1290383
24	60.96	34,0	93,2	75	19.81290383	1000	264.172051
25	63.50	35,0	95,0				
26	66.04	36,0	96,8				
27	68.58	37,0	98,6				
28	71.12	38,0	100,4				
29	73.66	39,0	102,2				
		40,0	104,0				

16102554R10044

Printed in Great Britain
by Amazon